Great and Small

Tucked within large symphonic movements, a crystalline intimacy shimmers. Josh Dugat's poems reveal the smarting, tender details that constellate this messy and gorgeous and terrifying and wonder-haunted existence. *Great and Small* is a remarkable book that conjures light from the spaces between absence and presence—it is a light that illuminates the path.
—Selah Saterstrom, author of *Ideal Suggestions* and *Slab*

The poems in Josh Dugat's *Great and Small* are as playful in language as they are heart shaking in implication. I appreciate this poet for the way he keenly observes the things of this world in one hand while grasping toward the wider meanings with the other.
—Carrie Fountain, author of *Instant Winner* and *The Life*

It's always struck me as a highest aspiration for poetry to yearn after, what William Wordsworth called "some philosophic Song / Of Truth that cherishes our daily life." In *Great and Small*, Josh Dugat sings toward the very ideal of that philosophic song, cherishing our daily life in poems of rich music and delicate rhyme. Alive to the conundrums that riddle our contemporary world—anxious technologies, lamentable injustices— Dugat's poems also pulse with mythic precedent. So it is, despite a sober-eyed, fatherly look at contemporary culture, these poems veer away from the ease of critique into ground both rarer and worthier: they take upon themselves the work of praise. It's hard work, praise. The mind feels a strange responsibility to think itself toward misery, but here, in these wonderful pages, the intelligence is what learns to tremble with joy.
—Dan Beachy-Quick, author of *Circle's Apprentice*

Josh Dugat's *Great and Small* is a first book, and its variety shows the all-roads-at-once exuberance that characterizes debut volumes. What makes *Great and Small* so interesting is that most of those roads lead to the southern landscapes of Dugat's childhood and current life. He evokes his everyday world with crafty intelligence and gentle lyricism. The book has many poems, all quite different, that surprised me, such as "Six Months before Marriage," "Bookmarks," "Rodeo," or "Setting the Leaf in My Grandmother's Table." Each made some moment of consciousness, great or small, unforgettable.
—Dana Gioia, author of *Meet Me at the Lighthouse* and *99 Poems*

Most readers will recognize the phrase "great and small" from the television show, *All Creatures Great and Small*, based on James Herriot novels, the title taken from a hymn setting of Psalm 104:24–25. The King James Version of these lines read: "O LORD, how manifold are thy works! in wisdom hast thou made them all: the earth is full of thy riches. / So is this great and wide sea, wherein are things creeping innumerable, both small and great beasts." In formally deft poems that often read like songs and prayers, Josh Dugat pays devotional, hoverfly attention to the full gamut of creation, from mustard-seed minutia (the "cat's blue pupil" of a gas pilot light or the "mica wings" of an insect caught in a windshield's crack) to sublime, leviathan immensities of nature, belief, and love (Goliath's "majestic" hands, the "abyssal plains" of a dying whale). A fetus grows in the immense and growing ocean of its mother's womb. Even large words hold smaller ones, ("listened/lists" and "vice/device"), and all realms—the great and small—exchange their secrets. This breviary of a debut collection offers lessons in how to live: "Burning / to be still. Patient / for the absences / we practice, fragrant / with our moisture / and our salt."

—Lisa Russ Spaar, author of *Madrigalia: New & Selected Poems* and *Paradise Close: A Novel*

The patient and potent poems of Josh Dugat's *Great and Small* scale both in the musical sense and in the architectural and geographical ones as well. They zoom from the minute to the massive, focused focus focusing. Dugat is a fine worrier of these worries, circling like Bishop, like Berry, rapt removed and moving in the updrafts of sensation, of sense, of sigh.

—Michael Martone, author of *Plain Air: Sketches from Winesburg, Indiana*

Great and Small

POEMS

BY

Josh Dugat

ABLE MUSE PRESS

Able Muse Press

www.ablemusepress.com

Printed in the United States of America

Names: Dugat, Josh, 1987- author.
Title: Great and small : poems / by Josh Dugat.
Description: San Jose, CA : Able Muse Press, 2024.
Identifiers: LCCN 2023008929 (print) | LCCN 2023008930 (ebook) |
  ISBN 9781773491370 (paperback) | ISBN 9781773491387 (ebook)
Classification: LCC PS3604.U3846 G74 2023 (print) | LCC PS3604.
  U3846 (ebook) | DDC 811/.6--dc23/eng/20230317
LC record available at https://lccn.loc.gov/2023008929
LC ebook record available at https://lccn.loc.gov/2023008930

Cover image: *Days Forgotten* by Kent Ambler

Cover & book design by Alexander Pepple

Able Muse Press is an imprint of *Able Muse: A Review of Poetry, Prose &
  Art*—at www.ablemuse.com

Able Muse Press
467 Saratoga Avenue #602
San Jose, CA 95129

Acknowledgments

Grateful acknowledgment is made to the editors of the following publications in which these poems, or earlier versions, first appeared:

America: "The Dumpster Fillers"

Barely South Review: "On Ross Dam"

The Christian Century: "The Orchid and the Wasp," "Six Months Before Marriage," "Hoverflies," "Recalling Yeats, Learning of the Mass Shootings in El Paso and Dayton, Rocking our Son Back to Sleep," "Mister Icarus," and "Screen"

Christianity and Literature: "The Welder"

Cider Press Review: "Setting the Leaf in My Grandmother's Table"

The Dead Mule School of Southern Literature: "Fossil"

Floyd County Moonshine: "How I Come to Bare," "Late December, Lavaca County"

The Literary Review: "Spile"

The Merton Seasonal: "Notes Recovered from a Search for Sanctity"

The Ocotillo Review: "Close Your Eyes" (as "Learning Braille")

Pinyon: "Burial of Bonnie and Clyde"

Reunion: The Dallas Review: "Dance Lessons"

Texas Poetry Calendar (2023): "Planter's Pantoum"

Tiny Seed Literary Journal: "Last Call at the Bees' Spring Saloon"

TriQuarterly: "Clamming for Clams"

The Watershed Review: "Beloved Gray Whale Dies after Fifty-Three Days in the Klamath River," "Kessler Koi Pond, Lavaca County," and "Road to Damascus"

"Hyphae/Hyphens" was published as a limited series of artist books in collaboration with Frog Song Press.

Thank you, thank you to the many hearts and minds that strengthened these poems and this poet through the years of their making. To my parents, Bill and Kathy, and my brother, Will, for surrounding me in story, song, and prayer. The same can be said of my grandparents, and the generations and generations before them.

To the places that have raised and shaped me, especially Austin, the Kessler Ranch, New Orleans, Alabama.

O my lucky stars! To my beloveds of the Compound, for your creative example and love, especially Nico, Ray, Cort, Stefin, Carrie, Joel, Aimee, Michael and Michael. Hicks, your friendship and affirmation of the writing life has buoyed me across the years. Thank you.

To Cindy Gelb, for the love and support of August and Edie that made finishing this collection possible.

To the writers and teachers who have offered light along the way, Sam and Sally Green, Michael Morse, Rick Kenney, Karen Kevorkian, Greg Orr, Jennifer Horne, Joel Brouwer, Robin Behn, Dan Beachy-Quick, Dana Gioia, Carrie Fountain, Selah Saterstrom, and especially Lisa Russ Spaar, Michael Martone, L. Lamar Wilson, and Heidi Lynn Staples.

To Sarah Scarr and Jillian Sico, for a real spirit of collaboration and creation.

To Kent Ambler for *Days Forgotten*.

To Alex and Carina and Able Muse Press for belief in these poems and the care to share them.

To August and Edie, you teach me and amaze me every day. Thank you.

To Nicole, again, and always. Soft in my speech, soft in my thoughts, everything, everything, by and by.

Contents

Great and Small

Great and Small

Close Your Eyes

The word you feel is *shell*. Lift it
from the paper. Let it roll down
to the well of your palm, and rest.

You know this shell. Brittle spire,
body whorl the length of bone
inside your fingertip. Maroon and spotted

outer lip. Twelve spirals turning
over shoulder, suture—hog's tooth
and a china bell. Scale its weight

by laying your tongue slack
inside your mouth. Name it: *Juno's Volute.*
Place it back. Maybe a chitinous flake

will stick, a skeleton silk
strung from the garment
of a still-living animal.

Kessler Koi Pond, Lavaca County

There was no thought of China's Yellow River
when my mother, and my father with her,
unspooled a school of fry into the trough.
Nor had they maps of myths to tie the oft-

inscripted drama of that cousin-
fish—who fought the fall's wet bludgeon
to its top, then looking down on tumbling gallons
grew gill-lungs and sprung wings of a dragon.

My parents only wanted to depose
the algal matts that greened and choked the flow
of water for the cattle. And it worked—
tens of carp lips chewed and swallow-slurped

the scummy bloom. The pool grew translucent.
Cow tongues lapped their scaled and undulant
reflections into full-flown fins, and then,
one by one, they left the trough abandoned.

Where did they go, the fish that labored long
for us? We didn't know, until the yawn
of a Mexican eagle bid us higher,
eyeing which past life she'd next lift skyward.

Dance Lessons

I learned to dance by standing
on my mother's feet, pretending
that our kitchen was the smoke-
filled Broken Spoke. The ceiling

was as low. The dish soap
and Diet Coke played forty-two
with coupons for their dominoes.
They stopped to watch us lope

across the brick to London
Homesick Blues. My fingers clung
onto her belt loops when she spun
me, set me down and sang

the line that taught my legs to match:
step-together, step-touch, step-back.
I outgrew my boots. My partner
dropped me off at homecoming—

a whole swollen gymnasium
of children playing mothers,
trying to tell each other's
bodies what to do. The lights

returned their childhoods, half-
turned. I waited by the punch
alone. She picked me up
and brought me home.

Spile

Unwrapped, it was the length
        and heft of a house
key: hollow, gray, quick to sip
        heat from my palm.

It could have been a pipe, or a whistle.
        I held it with my lips
to read your last translation
        of what we'd grow to say,
breathing notes like water
        nearly boiling in a kettle.

        The spile was used to draw sap out, one of three
                stuck in the sides of a great sugar maple. Ten gallons
        flowed through its stem, to be simmered
                in a shack into one thick, arterial quart of black syrup.

This one had broken, so could be sent.

I rub the injured end, skinned knee
        scabbed with tiny crystals, cool as granite—
place the whole tool inside my mouth.

I don't find metal's bloody tang.
        My tongue is dumb, only feels the shape of taste—
white ice, sugar water, salt
        on your neck from beneath your scarf.

If only Apollo knew—he could use Cupid's
        dull tip on Daphne again, during day between freeze and thaw,
find the laurel's ample phloem—just before the heartwood—
        and tap.

Hyphae, Hyphens

Will-o'-the-wisp's
whisked ligaments, needle-
frond instructions singing

separate beads of words
as one. One body's warmth
beneath the bedding's

overgrowth, vining
warp and weft, enfolding
lonesome feet. The give

and take of wanting
to say two things at once.
Sweet-bitter. Forget-me-

not. Hypodermic sting
of muscle's memory, line drawn
taut between the reel and pike,

keeling in the green-grey deep.
Ribboned dragon strung
around the wrist, it lifts and dives

against the grey-green sky.
Severance is a luscious risk
the recluse spins. Precarious—

the diving bell's umbilicus,
measurement of breathlessness—
your toe hair brushing mine.

Mister Icarus

The house was, what—a quarter-mile away
	from ours? Elm and green St. Augustine,
two-car mirage. Assortment of machines
	built to persuade weeds with blades. And an airplane.
Well, the start of one—a wooden bird
	born bones-first and growing, rib by moonward
rib. A pterodactyl skeleton.
	A cage to wrap an angel in.

Whose permission are you waiting for?
	How long will you not risk plummeting,
leaving someone else's hero to the summiting?
	The neighbors—let the neighbors stir.
The grave can have its gravity.
	One bright day, and the garage was empty.

Six Months Before Marriage

Inside the book you have been given, questions
throw sharp light upon mice that stir beneath
the cabinet trim: *If we are infertile, what then?*
How will we both care for our ailing parents?
       Coarse frost crawls and fractures

into hope of knowing: cold will only
draw us toward each other, ever tightly.
When you read, *What arrangements would you choose*
for your memorial? briefly, I must
       bury you—I don't

know how. You say you want to rest beneath
a fruiting tree, for shade and something sweet to give—
have your ashes mixed with loam, and spread amongst
the roots. I say I would gladly join you there.
       Later, this evening,

when you're dreaming, I lean over you to turn
off your bedside lamp. Pausing, I kiss your hair-
line, my bottom lip upon your snowy forehead,
nose over your scalp. Already, you've begun
       to taste like peaches.

Bookmarks

I use things that have lost their use:
his save-the-date, now overdue,
our power bill, paid late, but paid.

I lose these too, then mark my page
with dog-ears, or, what's worse (*tsk, tsk*)—
I chicken scratch. I asterisk.

It did not always come to this.
The spine still bears the vestiges
of books' embryogenesis

when tails unfurled like basilisks
from Coptic Codex coccyxes.
A relic on a classicists'

hermetic shelf. The ribbons fray.
They come unbound and fall away.
Unremarkable as lint,

the osprey threads her ornament.
A remnant snatched. The pack rat chews.
And here—here's something left to lose.

Kitchen Poem

You ask for a funnel.
It's been on your list

since we last sat down
and decided this

was the way
we were going

to change things.
We bought little

notebooks—notebooks
that caked into pucks

in our pockets
when I washed our pants.

*What will help you
remember?* you ask

(your soft admonition).
I write reminders

on Post-its stuck
next to the trash.

Lists on the fridge,
on the mirror, the dash.

Lists like prayer flags
with *x*'s and boxes

unchecked. Exhausted,
we stopped making

lists. We just listened,
and sensed that we knew

what the other would
pray. We both stayed

quiet. I wish,
when you pour

long-simmered stock,
hot and strong,

from our giant
steel pot

into a small-
mouthed bottle,

I had the one thing
you asked for

to offer.

Abraham Binds Isaac

Is sin, sin?
Is one in seven?

Soon, son,
soon. O

son. No
vice. Vine-

noose. O vision—
son-in-oven.

Vie, veins.
Vie neon sense—

O visive noise,
divine envoi—

one ovine nose.

Fossil

Black Warrior River

It is a mammoth
lily pad. A trash can
lid. A great armored bubble
bobbing in the river, unable
to birth itself
from the surface. No,
it is a turtle—
what the first reflexive thought
thought, before logic
guffawed, the artifact found
clownishly immense for an animal
not yet extinct. *Did you forget to die
with the other dinosaurs?* She will answer.

Closer, she is spined
with ancient knuckles. I wave another
angler over. I have never
seen so big a turtle
in the wild, if the wild is where
we are, here, between the dam
and pier. He has not either. She rocks with flushes
yawning from the weir, her head down
like a snorkeler intent upon a star
lodged within a reef. A piece of garbage
sticks behind her, bagged and brightly
veined. She doesn't seem to mind,

14

even though the bag is one of her
soft organs and she is not held by a star,
but by a line
fixed deeper than we see. I have hung
up here too. Cut my lines and left them,
unthinking of their hazard.

I did not forget
to die, her body tells us.

The moving water does her swimming
for her. We lay on our stomachs,
reach with sticks and catch her
tether, tug her. Now we smell her,
yellow, sour, easing toward us
like a beehive best left sleeping.
She wears claws like jewelry.
She was a warrior-priestess
or a queen.
He holds her by the ankles and I try
to lift her head. Taut, I touch
my knife beneath her chin—
the filament relents. He hefts her
greening gallons from the water,
falling to the pier. She rests.
Is she smaller, now, and hideous,
or just as grand, and sadder?
She could not snap the line
with all her razors. That flinted beak
cracked open, edges wasted
pleading with the shallows for a breath.

How many hours did she hold it?
Hind parts parched, shell hot
as an island, cool at night.
Her fossil eyes
lost in the wet
where there was a worm
or shiner just like any other,
and now nothing
but strange pain inside, and
wonder. In the drug of drowning
could you see yourself as we do,
Tangled Angel? Stepping stone
from here to after,
that we may use your back
to get where we are going,
keeping
our feet dry.

Lightning Tree, Lavaca County

The robins saw it—
            shower's splinter
      swallowed by the post oak,
hollowing the trunk into a cello
you could bury a small boy in.
            At night the ulcer glowed,
                  spreading in my sleep,
            crowning limbs in light and leaping
over perching birds and
sleeping boys. Wildfire's
            embryo, untended.
                  Where it spreads. How it grows.
            I was the only one to worry,
wet as winter ended.
In weeks, I warmed
            to what it was
                  we kept—a pet
eternal flame, chained inside
a tree. My brother and I craned
to read the whispering
            smoke. The cursive in the canopy
                  confounded, never spelled
            how brush could start, stay lit so long
and not become consumed.
We almost didn't hear it. Did we?
            Embers hissing
                  one long wish aloud—
      either *put,* or *let*
                        me out.

Pilot Light

Only hint at just how dark the kitchen is—
cat's blue pupil, pin-shaped pinhole,
slit in the eyeball's backside,
semaphore, camera, mirror-flash, maypole
streamer strung on end, whispering ribbon
snake, figure skater dazzled
in her own cosmic inertia, chthonic top
locked inside a stovetop's iron mask (stew-
rusted, chili-greased, tecton ossified and cut
by petrologists' diamond bits, unearthing what the
ancients fried for supper), other lamp
of the tabernacle, Espiritu Santo, Vanuatu-blue,
white-blue like light leaked from deep-
sea vents, light that invents photosynthesis
in heat-bent bacteria, light felt not seen,
far right of visibility, where anglerfish dangle
hideous underbites, where submarine hulls groan
and give in, wheeze valve-hisses, tend pipes
that send gasps of the earth's
nine-chambered heart
past bones of pliosauruses,
past mammoth duff still dank and dandered, still
stuck in permafrost, up
to the hungry surface
where a billion geodesic carbon dice
roll from spires of a Gulf Coast refinery,
cairn the horizon and mark the end
of sight, of sky, of something, floating
into the midnight kitchen, where blue blows
icy and incessantly, listing in a gust
and snapping to.

Goliath

My hands refuse to hide their size
but they can knit a dress majestic—
ring on ring, the sequins sheathe
my chest, and yes, protect
you from the heart-shaped lock inside.
I exhaust myself to look electric.
My shining legs. I polish everything
your eyes cannot stop measuring.

I want a king. I want someone
to wear something just for me,
to strut his love uncircumscribed.
To want to touch me. Don't you, lovely?
Is that too much? I would let my hair down
for you to climb, just to hear you say good morning—
let my armor glamorize the ground,
wake up rocking in your sling, safe and sound.

Rodeo

West Feliciana Parish

Every Sunday in October
stock and riders wear a number.
Crowds astride the bleacher lumber
search the suited cowboys over

figuring they will discover
something marking us from other.
Every Sunday in October
stock and riders wear a number.

Some are young, and some are older.
A man chews catfish, hot and tender,
burns his tongue and puffs still-summer
air to make his numb tongue number,
on a Sunday, in October.

Burial of Bonnie and Clyde

When it came time to die,
they ran whooping from the life
they'd loved to trick, laid down
in a ditch and closed their eyes,
tried to stifle breathing
through their smiles.

It tickled when their bones
were picked. They pursed their lips,
clutched giggles until Earth
had nudged and sniffed,
stood watch, grown bored,
and sauntered on.

Charlie Dreams of Changing

Boy: *What right, cardinal,*
do you have to be
so bright?

Bird: *I have survived*
by scarletting.

Boy: *How do you see*
past the mask
that darks your eyes?

Bird: *Son, some colors evanesce.*
Some magnetize.

And look! A sunflower
gone to seed!

Boy: *I wish you would*
lift time from my shoulders,
even for a moment.

Bird: (crunching seeds)

Feathers started
as an accident
to insulate cold blood

from the cold. Angels needed
wings for warmth
before they stumbled into flight.

Last Call at the Bees' Spring Saloon

They do not even wait for the season
to rise from his bed, button his buttons—
bright-belled and petaled with crisp, pleated leaves on.
The bees barely sit until one sudden

brush of the sun's bow awakens stiff strings—
just a thin dust of pollen for rosin,
and limbs start remembering swinging.
The dive warming up, no bee has forgotten

her steps. That hive of a jukebox keeps time.
Wing upon wing of the one golden hit
every sister grew singing inside. Each line
sweetly hummed, long after the band quits

again, and she's left—the lights all turned down—
to lose herself in the soft song and the crowd.

Pineapple

Denuded of cactaceous plume
and chainmail quilt, the fruit
transudes canary juice. Lamp
inside a cuttlefish, more citrus
than coniferous, more butter,
now, than barnacle. Tart neon
ingot. Geode's saccharine yoke.

The planter knows how order
can be forced. It is an ordinary
story. He fails to cede dominion
of a plan, and the orchard is
plantationed. Prone to doom
or profit, in some order. Or,
at least, to root knot nematodes.

Rule and regulation. Rank.
Religious discipline. *Order*
also shares a root with *ordiri*—
"begin to weave," perhaps,
as in, *primordial*, or the Proto-
Indo-European, *ar* — "to fit
together." *Art* and *harmony*.

I am not an etymologist.
I have grown exactly one
pineapple, more or less
haphazardly. That's the wrong
attribution of agency—
I have watched one pineapple
grow itself, more or less, exactly.

Peacock of the produce aisle,
bought (half off!) and chopped
for something domestic/exotic.
Smoothies. Guacamole.
Slip and sucker could be cut
and planted, you had read,
whatever slips and suckers are.

Ditto crowns. I buried one
inside a pot, an inch or so of flesh
below the cowlick, not expecting
much. Watered through the summer,
spiked aqueducts deflected
rivulets into adjacent terra cotta.
Indoors in November, our kitchen-

cum-terrarium, our crowded
paupers' tropics. We moved houses,
it moved with us. Three years
growing, and—just this fall—a flower!
Not one flower, mind you, but
an *inflorescence*. Pom-pom prehistoric,
popsicle with tentacles! Beautiful

in newness and in always
having been. A jeweled grenade
whose seeded scales align
in sequence, Fibonacci
would have noticed, needless
of the cultivator's weld, or even
of his noticing. Whistling

the theme and variation
requires some attention
to the seasons. Order loosely held,
less grip than guide. Permission
to submit to the vertiginous
assemblage of shape exploding
out of Byzantine mosaic tesserae.

The Orchid and the Wasp

As the male wasp nuzzles forward in his attempts to mate, he butts
the pollinia, which stick to him like yellow horns.
   — David Attenborough, The Private Life of Plants

She does not promise that her purfle fur
is fur, or vouch the truth of her perfume.
Such details don't consume the bachelor
who consummately longs to be the groom.
The honey bees ply less impassioned trips
across her garden of delights. So do flies,
who neither fall for ultraviolet lips
nor slip upon the hem of her disguise.

But the wasp's desire blinds. He thrusts
the hips of his decoy mistress, heedless
of her will. And she, foreseeing of his lust,
resolves to use his rutting head in secret.
It isn't that he gets what he deserves.
The orchid bides so beautifully, it hurts.

On Ross Dam

How much water must gather
        for a body
to become another body? You and I
        are small as birds
                in the basket of the North Cascades
and my breath catches
        to see the terns
plummet below us,
        one thousand feet
                along the curved thumbnail
that holds the whole Skagit
        back. Downriver there is a house
where turbines draw
        flecks of power from the water
                like a prospector. In two nights
we will be in Seattle,
        with Ben and Michael and
your brother, where all the gold
        glows on display. The gray waves
                on Ross Lake cannot imagine
they will be stopped
        where we are standing, changed
into another kind
        of wave. We cannot
                help but wonder
how the dam will one day
        give way, enjoining us
into a current as sudden

and cold as a mountain. The canyon promises
        the concrete, despite its youth
and tensile strength, that it is already
        washing away, grist by grain. You are twelve weeks
pregnant and peering at the terns
        as they wheel above the rocks,
                riding the lip of the wind back up
to play in every pocket of sky
        the dam has found
for them. Your hands are on your hips
        and your back is to the lake. You turn
                to see if I felt it too, these vibrations
underneath our feet, that groan
        to stave off any breach, and long to
age like the cliffs
        of basalt, to let
                the water fall
and break.

The Welder

The mask is lowered. In the dark,
an acrid singe attends a spark
that showers the periphery
and starts the metal liturgy.

The craftsman undertakes to guide
the arc and so discharge completely.
Past and current rectified—
BC/AD, AC/DC.

Less than stainless atoms strung
in steely bonds join the elect-
rons pouring from a flaming tung-
sten tip. A noble gas protects

them. Then, the lake of fire cools
into a wounded-palm-sized pool.
The scale is moot. He blinks eclipse.
He lifts the veil—apocalypse.

Figure Study

Isadora died in spectacular fashion
the Graces themselves had made with their labor.
Her satin contrail caught in the axle
and wrested a last, Attic act of sedition.

She recast Corinthian temples with nipples
unshrinking and sandals abandoned, exhausted
the postures paraded by nature and skipped
at the prospect of bad affectation.

Mad as a lover, the silk plucks the dancer,
impressing her throat like the calm muscled hand
of a sculptor. Dusk for the dimmed solar plexus

and ash, ash—sparkle like marble. Suspended,
did you see her move? Limbed and Winged?
Victorious, bloodless, and breathless?

Infernal Dactyls

I.

Thadius Abacus
Brutus and Cassius
sat on the portico
biting their nails.

If you can trust Virgil's
meteorology,
even the sky appeared
ready to hail.

II.

Pickory Rosary
Judas Iscariot
stared at his supper but
didn't say much.

Only his wife knew his
irreconcilable
silence. She kissed him and
he spilled his guts.

Loom

The Odyssey, Book 2: 119–121

Weaving and unweaving her gorgeous web,
the queen's thread snared stares across her closet room.
We knew the words but held them in our heads:

the king is dead. Or, speechless now, is kept
on ventilations by a sighing loom,
weaving and unweaving the gorgeous web.

Starved for sleep, shed bid us, dumb from bed
to lift her heddle, to pass the shuttle through.
We learned her words and held them in our heads—

how voice itself might spell away the dread
of glaring day. Unmute, we grew consumed
with weaving and unweaving gorgeous webs.

Treason, unkind history has said,
but also said: *I spoke*. Seduced by truth—
the gorgeous, new unweaving of a web.
The words I knew and loosed beyond my head.

Hippocampus spp.

To start—
a Spanish question
mark that floats
before the quest-
ion. A treble clef,
flipped bishop's
crook or fiddlehead
—now let me stop.
We sort top down, or else
end up upended. Blame gravity,
judiciously. Moon rocks don't know
north from Adam's off ox. Jesus' toe
rings, haloes too. Footwasher,
baptizer. Last shall be first.
In Old Norse, the head
word and determinant
switch seats at will—
the kenning's sense still sticks.
In any case, *bender fender* says it better. End
over end, distance thinned into
a dent. Homologous struc-
tures lack strict
referents.

A fish
skull is no more
a horse's than
the other way
around. We work
with what we know.
Get this: in some
teleosts, the forebrain
is inverted relative to other
vertebrates. Medial is lateral and
vice versa. You cannot make this up.
Blame natural selection, especially.
The seahorse father gives birth—
as if duality and nonduality
were the only ends
of one spectrum.
My centaur is a mer-
fern, named for neither extremity.
Have you seen the ponies swim from Chincoteague?
Nostrils puffing salt at slack tide.
Heads like birds above the
water, ears for wings. It
is something.

Birmingham Botanical Garden

A mockingbird
hops to a bench, says
nothing. My child is still

four months
from his birth.
I am trying

to resist talking, even though
I'll always want
to ask what you are thinking

if thinking
is what you are nearly doing
in the growing ocean

of your mother. Without
my glasses, I read
the sign beside the trailhead:

*Parents, Please Surprise
Your Children.*
Closer, and I clarify,

Supervise,
to no one
but myself,

and hear
my silence
mocked.

Text and Drive

Are you this aching to connect
to scratch before you feel the itch
a myoclonic motor tic
a traffic thumb stop rubberneck
predictive script autonomous
quick limbic hit kiss dopamine
a bird into a window screen
a broken wing a loneliness.

Found on Google Street View

Franklin and N. Robertson, New Orleans

Watch the streetlights change,
    shadows shift ninety degrees.

Letters rearrange
    on the Burger King marquee:

    2 FOR $5 WHOPPER FISH
        CHICKEN   PULLPORK
inflates to
        2 FOR $6
The vacant school adverts

a still-expectant promise
    on an anachronous sign

stranded since an August:
    STUDENT   RETURN
        2005

Tags crop up like cat's-claw
    on electric boxes—

Paper bags with Mad Dog
    bottles burst. A blossom winks.

White keys of the crosswalk
    play their way around the cracks

to whatever track the pickup
        driver whistles driving past.

David flies his cardboard
        four years before his stroke,

his blue eyes that afford
        to fix yours, Reader (*Read* it!)—BROKE

Screen

Every night you scan the news,
the black and white, the red, the bruise

that cannot lighten when backlit.
The battery does not relent.

You made your bed, now this mistake—
device does not a vice unmake.

It spews the day's vicissitudes.
It vies. It lets bad visions through.

Your feed has made a wound afresh
and tender now, as words make flesh.

Starved, you stuff the open sore
with more of what you read. And more.

The hours pass. You look around.
Or die for lack of what is found.

Recalling Yeats, Learning of the Mass Shootings in El Paso and Dayton, Rocking Our Son Back to Sleep

The lips of the angels
Blister and flame.
Their mouthpieces painful
From trumpeting name

After name. They lay down
Their horns and the dead
Still arrive, dying to drown
Out the hush in their heads

That would crush paradise.
You have their hymns
In your skin memorized,
Spilling your lungs and your limbs.

You don't sleep. You don't sleep.
Your delicate chest
How it wails and it weeps
That overcome angels might rest.

Late December, Lavaca County

The deer forget their breath
behind them when they run; a rush of warmth
that late December carves
up quick and grays in its white bark.

We watch from the porch,
both hands on the cup, the sweet-
hay steam of tea barely
brushing your chin before freezing.

These are the mammal months
and we are the tallest ornaments
on the tree. Bundled, we walk to the pens
where the bulls count their hours

or just ruminate. The five sandy Herefords:
shoals of muscle so much older
than the blonde and drowsy curls
upon their brows. They are boys, especially

the raccoon-eyed one Carl calls his pet.
I wonder what it might mean to a bull
to be a favorite, and if they have
a favorite too. Do you? The Brahma—

pronounced *Bramer* for as long
as I remember—stands smoky-hided
and a head above the rest. He wears
his pointed ears like vestments

of a priest who dresses every morning
even though his shape of God
will always be misshapen. They are quiet,
each of them, and the trough beside the fence

is dry. The pipe that feeds it sprays
like an artery that might paint
its own cold rainbow. Puddles mud in postholes
that the bulls have punched. Did the freeze

cause the pipe to bust? Or was it
their orneriness, allowing you and I
to think that animals as big as them
might be in need of us. We shut the water

off, drag a hose and fill the trough
back up. It might be ice by morning,
which seems a long way off.
Time doesn't slow, so much as tighten,

huddled from the broader planes
of spring or fall—if you stand here
you can see it, all at once, drawn together
in a chord that stings when it is struck.

Squeamish

It's not the blood that freaks
but the bloodlessness. The heart cracks

like spaghetti squash. There's no nice
word for worm.

They only get worse—cad and creep.
The ones you cannot see.

In muscled husks they writhe, plum-
colored. Gel for meat.

When most folks get this close, they shriek
or heave. Expect a smell, remember

rhymes about pinochle.
But you hold out your pinkie,

let one wrap around you,
shying from bright, vying

for the quiet cup of your palm.
You hold it there, as in prayer,

and say how fine a house I've built,
our flocks and herds have multiplied,

how I have not forgotten the Lord
who brought us out of Egypt.

Planter's Pantoum

45

To choose the ground for beds
you watched the light for weeks.
How soon the morning spread
to noon, its ebbs and peaks.

You watched the light for weeks.
You saw tulips salute
to noon. The ebbs and peaks
that call the coming fruit.

You saw tulips salute.
We made rows by the street.
The call of coming fruit
displayed. And grayed defeat.

We laid rows by the street.
A tender shoot bouquet
displayed. And grayed defeat
delayed another day.

How I Come to Bare

At night, dizzy irises succumb
to lulling from a resting sun.
A drafty house and deeds undone
set an itching conscience
rolling. I fold my quilts in mittened hands,
inhale an ember of stove air
and head out into ochre light,
sighed by glacial constellations.

The ground gives way beneath
each boot, the sound of bird bones
breaking. Tender as a fisher
casting nets, I lay blankets
on the broccoli, dill, the winter greens,
the pretty lips of budding beets. A few
gone gray from evening's freeze.
A few already lost.

When every carried layer's placed,
and onion shoots still bend, unclothed,
my numb hands fumble buttonholes,

I tuck my cotton shirt around them—
pant leg on each radish row,
a sock upon a parsnip top.

And so I come to stand
before the things I've grown in nothing
more than skin

which I might also give
to save that which
I'll take in time.

Beloved Gray Whale Dies after Fifty-Three Days in the Klamath River

Light fights hard, shattering plankton to asters. Invisible skin

hinders descent—below us it's dark

as an animal's inside. From viscera of mid-sea

trenches, abyssal plains, rise fibrils strung with pearls of air—

wishes loosed by lovers.

★

In the time between a cry and its echo, the island falls.
Ashes cast to ocean, only prolonging

the return of sound. We wait, salt
cakes on our faces—elegies get stuck in our heads, become hackneyed.

We repeat years, and speak less—mindful of wearing thin the only words we know.

After the augurs say

what we guessed they would, we sleep like dogs,

our legs ever ambling—
a sleep that in waking, we can't help but run from.

★

After such movement, and so many days, the breadth of our memory
sheers—horizon bruised by a paling sun. We call our own lungs

into question. How have the atoms,
              in tedious constancy, not grown restless
                    with revolt?
                                      There is sweetness left:
scent of calf hide and kidskin. His breath when dreaming.

Stamp of solace—or something
      close to love—cut firmly in the leather of the life we've lived.

★

You will die in the river, they say, and we smile. So do the salmon. They know
      when to go home. If we have windows, we will roll
them down. If we have drums, or chests and fists, we will be noisemakers. If we do not—

we will find another way.   This is our attempt—our bighearted demolition
        of the full body casts   that shed, may be shattered and spread
to make bedrock for beaches   and soft pillowed ground

                          for the feet of two people
                            to walk and run on.

Stone Eater

Scientists have long assumed the stones help the semiaquatic reptiles digest prey; a new study suggests they also enable the crocs to spend more time submerged.
— National Geographic, *August 2019*

You will have heard about the jaws—
ferocious in their closure,
held shut with a touch.

You will not have heard
the infrasound, but might have
seen the quaverings

unnerving bayou's surfaces
and quaking the canoe hull.
Pebble in the gut's shoe

reminds the mind
what not to do.
Sit with that sinking-

stomach feeling, Poet.
Charon, or a friend,
takes you by the wrist

and holds a scaly finger
to your lips. *Shhhh,*
she says. *It's for the best.*

Sticks and stones may break
but words are never
painless to be eaten.

Clamming for Clams

After ten years, recollection's net
        needs mending. I tie in nylon,
                replacing torn sections, but that is all I know
of how to slow forgetting. Recall the kelp
        in clumps and strands
like God's oleaginous green
        hair clogging our shower drain.

Slurp of sand gulping the shovel down—
        four cuts framing little exhalations,
                sparkling and vanishing. From each upheaval,
we plucked shut fortune cookies,
        plunked them in the bucket.
Innards gummed the blade.
        Intent on forms, I skewered contents.

My reckless digging didn't lessen—
        all dull skill and skull muscle.
                Eagles swarmed the beach behind us,
garrulous as gulls, and grateful,
        I imagined, to make use
of our mess. Birds of prey
        playing the gleaners. Call them

what you will. I project. We made
        a minefield. I project, still. We left
                for supper—clams with rosemary
and lemon. I am improficient
        at repair. I am reaching
for a better way to praise
        the soft parts.

Notes on an Inscription

At the National Memorial for Peace and Justice in Montgomery, Alabama, three people are named as victims of terror lynchings in Lavaca County, Texas. Louis Foster was murdered October 18, 1883. Bascom Cook and Lon Hall were murdered June 12, 1894.

to Lon Hall

The steel in which your name is cut
is red. Not rescued-from-the-fire-red,
not red-already-charred-and-cooled,
but red as textured light, light held
at the edge of what I am learning

to see. Your name in front of me.
Rust grows in slow rosettes. Here a calyx,
here a crown. Only rust to those of us
stuck peering for ourselves in safely
distant mirrors. One hundred years

can sound like history, if you let it.
Today, you were young, and June's
sweat burned in your eyelids'
lower furrow, making it hard to see
the ball you struck hard anyway.

Touch sparks sight. Vision with
or without light. Little fits of breeze,
grass-sweet from all the pasture's grasses,
all their stages: stem and seed,
chewed and shat. Hot, sweet summerbreath.

Before the next play, your brother
plucks a sticker burr from the ball.
You sip water, sand-sieved. Sweet.
Two roseate spoonbills clear their croaky throats,
too far away to see, but you see them anyway.

Eight months will bring a blizzard, burying the coast
in twenty inches, but that is far away, or feels it,
peering at the record that is kept. A game to follow church,
I read, the second time I find your name, behind the glass,
on microfilm, where text occludes the light and makes a story.

*The fearful affray out on Rocky reached here
Sunday evening.* A group of white boys stopped
and *a disturbance arose*, the story reports,
as if by some bad luck. You held a boy.
Another struck him with a yoke. The story

calls you Lou. The story gives little
chance for the struck boy's recovery.
You and your brother are never caught
in local print. That is the account of it.
The story runs two days after you are murdered.

I am learning how a story is maintained
on microfilm: a master negative is kept secured
from which service copies (positive) are made
for public use. A poem is a service copy
(positive) susceptible to scratches

and to noise. No. It speaks within the spaces
of the negative, which itself is not the story,
just a shadow, evidence of something
having happened, and of light.
I am learning

the heart is the size of the fist,
nothing new, except now the inverse must
be true. You give your knuckles gifts
of beating, just as branching arteries
beat. One heart for each hand, warm against

the shoulders of a boy. I am learning
the bird I always called a buzzard is in fact a kind
of vulture. All the names are rusting. Red cedar
is a juniper. Oak is manifold: post, red,
live, burr. Bark as thick as biscuit dough. Rust as rose.

The paper in Venita, Oklahoma doesn't name the tree:
it is reported that you are arrested
but taken from the officers. By whom? Everyone knew
everyone. The only neighbor's rope I knew
was kindness. We had a tire swing, tied to a limb

that could hold as many cousins as could hold
one another without letting go. The tree groaned,
and we grinned at playing what the wind did, making great
gray branches sway. The swing is gone, but not the limb.
Rubbed bald. No. A negative. I am learning

how roots send messages, receive them. Fungal threads
holding one another without letting go. Touch.
With or without light. Nothing new, except one tree
is not tidily one tree any longer. Never was. Same sun,
now as then. Tireless aperture, summer's pulsing stone

still showering the place that sees you—
what place could not see you—
here, where the ball rolls to the road,
and you slide past your brother, safe
at home.

At 6 a.m., the Tinman

lifts the daybreak's silence from the curbside,
alongside bike spokes, stove pipes, broken
chain link chattering his trailer tailgate.
The sun has not yet blinked, still warm and dreaming

of the morning she will make. Unspoken
Alchemist of Garbage Day, you see states
of matter not as fact, but teeming
with a thousand wings. The heart can only hide

so long from what it will become. I separate
aluminum and leave my weak redeeming
to a stranger. All you have beatified—
trash and treasure, chaff and emmer, golden

cans that can't remember meaning
before emptying. And me. Outside,
you throw shimmer on the closing-open
world, ceaseless in its change and molten weight.

Attentative

These consonants
are ticklish—

eyelash on a fly
leg, blinking

out of reach.
Regret will nest

against the sills
of best-laid panes,

and still,
to care is to be human.

A slip of hand
lets slide a substitution—

fickle cells made sick,
or, well, made fitter.

It is hard to tell.
The doomsday

sayer's day comes due.
The sun comes up,

and no comeuppance.
Hallelujah.

Pan toots
his manic music

just for you
to dance and dance.

Hallelujah.

Casting the Stone

An ammonite's ghost is a flask,
and as hard—a shellacked fool's
gold cast of the body abandoned.

Mollusk chalk and coral dust
agglomerate and alter: karst and marble.
Every exhumation makes a hole.

The *o* of history is stuffed
with balled socks to keep it hushed,
to fake meaning of the sinking,

at least temporarily.
We robe mammoth bones
in flesh, as we do to all the dead,

guessing colors for their pelts
and temperaments. A monument
is not a memory, but mimics one,

which mimics bedrock in its supposed
sturdiness. Geology is mutable, Lyell said.
Even hulking femurs, disentombed

and first presumed to be the devil's
clever shovel-work. Catalogued and plaqued,
the skeleton becomes an artifact. Meek

beneath the museum-keeper's keep.
Squeak of field trip tennis shoes on tile.
Soundless shape that seeping minerals make.

Notes Recovered from a Search for Sanctity

*Founded in 1848, the Abbey of Our Lady of Gethsemani near
Bardstown, Kentucky was built in part through the labor of people
who were enslaved. In a letter to a neighboring planter in 1859,
then-Abbot Dom Eutropius agrees to pay a hundred dollars for the
work of a man in the construction of the church. The man's name was
Able.*

The very stones and beams are all befriended
By cleaner sun, by rarer birds, by lovelier flowers.
  — "A Letter to My Friends," Thomas Merton, 1941

*The very stones will cry out from the wall and the beam will respond
from the woodwork.*
  — Habakkuk 2:11

Cain said to his brother Abel,
    Let us go out to the field.

The field is what was here
    before the chapel. The world

was here before the field.
    It is hard to find a place

to hide from God. It is hard
    to find a place beyond the world.

There are at least two kinds
    of silences. Only one is permanent.

Only one can work to sanctify
        the others. That is a statement

of hope, not certainty. The greater silence
        knows more than the poet

ever will, and, in time, subsumes
        the poet and the lesser silences

unto itself. It is a cycle
        only inasmuch as it is helpful

to be understood as such.
        I barely understand

how brick is made. Sand
        and lime, water, clinker.

All winter, clay amends
        in silent labor. The ground

does not cry out. Maple wilts its skin
        to paper. Slick as meat, a shape slips

in the mold. To make a brick.
        To cast a stone. Your fingerprints

adorn the vertebrae and sternum
        of the church. And what else?

Glints of bee balm in the spring.
      Your sweat and knuckle hair,

chipped fingernails. The faintest
      folds in drying matter,

bending to your breathing—
      trace of morning's kiss

from your beloved, whistle on your lips
      leftover from the lilting

conversation with a killdeer. Something
      whispered to your brother.

Who gets to say what singing is
      and isn't? It is a statement of hope,

not certainty, to say something
      can be doing both at once.

Road to Damascus

On the drive back from Kentucky,
a couple dozen insect carcasses
are caught between the sharp lips
of my Jeep's cracked windshield.

Mica wings flap at eighty miles an hour
and unable to lift. There are approximately
nine hundred other spatters spread across the glass
and no two are the same: green and goldenrod;

the strange, hanging red of a nocturnal eye;
ogling faces like you find when you squint
at the moon. They explode so quietly.
Some will astonish you in their symmetry—

more blossom than bird shit, like the insect
calculated the whole angle of approach, intending
to daub a starry forget-me-not. It is difficult
to tell where one gut starts and ends, and the road

grows hard to see. I pull out the squeegee
at the Conoco, dripping with greasy suds,
thick and blue as a urinal cake. I can't
bring myself to erase them, this being

the brief memorial for the thousands
of things I cannot name. I drive more slowly
the rest of the way in the closing dark,
and leave the great stain there for days,

drying into crust, blinking through
the afternoons until I'm caught
inside the throat of an August downpour—
I twist my wipers on by instinct

and the caked shapes soften and begin
to fall like scales from my eyes
with the rain calling down to me by name
and proclaiming forthwith, *enough is enough.*

Setting the Leaf in My Grandmother's Table

Another Holy Day—the table cannot hold
      Creation as it is: the eight-month-old
enraptured with his reach; the toddler who paints
      with gravy; cake pans grinning through the faint
crow's feet that age has cut, now brimming with the cryst-
      al skins of chicken-fried steak; the eldest
great-grandson's loosened memory (this plate, this place,
      the man who consummated every grace,
this food unto our bodies and our bodies to
      Thy use); remembrance she leads us through.

Set the table as a bone is set. Separate
      the ends to make a space. Be delicate.
The table cannot hold, nor can the prayer
      or leaf, but who could pray for such repair,
         or such relief.

Magnolia Thief

May Day snow globe
wrenched from branch and hauled hip-high
the whole way home. My love,
you thieve the temporary
irresistibly. Blossom granted blissful hospice—
you prop the fondant goblet in a jam jar
near your supper plate. You swirl

and sip—*Mmmmmmmuscadine.*
You whiff again. *Big-bodied
pinot grigio.* You let the petals live
into their bucket lists: ostrich egg
on mescaline; self portrait of your rib cage
in a concave mirror; bone slipping flesh's little dress
just to see how good it fits. You move

your vase onto the coffee table, sniff—
Vidalia onion's longing
to be born a swan; a penguin chick's
full moon milk dream, colostrum-rich;
meringue's brain on cream's wedding day;
cemetery's lingerie. The bowl spills open,
floods the kitchen. Leather feathers

tingeing tan, soften and begin
to drop. A windmill's wilting
fronds. Grave as dove, St. Francis fills
the basin for his birds.
You make me stop
washing the dishes. *Come here,
you've got to smell this.*

Little Narcissus

Mist masks the bathroom mirror,
wash on canvas. He crawls nearer,
smears the glass, the image clearer

than the self he sees in either
of your eyes. First selves. Features
teaching him to recognize so beautiful a creature.

Village Creek Nursing Center

I watercolor now. Every neighbor
has a hobby that lets her do what she
is able with her aging body. Three
women gather Mondays in the cater-
cornered room, strewn with sterling tufts and crumbling
at the touch, winnowed from the locks still
strong enough to weave—a spinning mill
for shorn hair wreaths. Bare scalps plum and gleam
with light their faces can no longer hide
in folds, cloistered there since years and years ago.

Klara doesn't speak. With her teeth, she holds
an end of yarn, a pair of toothpicks tucked inside
her mouth. She casts on woolen fiber—right
needle through the first loop, purlwise.
She maneuvers a closed mouth with closed eyes,
seesaw brow and jaw, what she might
look like chewing pine cones with her gums.
Out grows her new knit tongue. She pats
it dry. Wet off-white with red-matte
marbling. A gift for someone's grandson.

As soon as I unclasp the brassen locket,
your picture's underwater—cool crib
of an open clam. The brush tip dips
into the shallow pool, a floret
bursts blue over you. With the next touch
you are purple, then dark brown. On paper,
your face mosses into colored vapor.
A thick fruit grows around you, and as much
as I try to paint away the layers,
I only ever lose you, little prayer.

When I Miss You in My Sleep

    Even the waves grow lost
among themselves,

        rolling in unknowing
circles; they wash

        their edges clean
of crest and cusp.

        They fold and rest,
lull the longing albatross

        through ivory dreams—
alone, adrift, aloft.

        Awoken by a sudden wind,
the downy memories

        still loop—silly
wooing: caw and call.

        Aching starts the long
arc home. It is the same

        for me. Every morning,
a returning, a burying

of oars, beholding little
scars that mark us:

strange woman,
strange man.

The Dumpster Fillers

They arrive at night, unseen
except for headlights splitting hedge.
All the other scenes are sounds—

arthritic door hinge, radio drowned
beneath the engine's windy idle.
A trunk yawns up. Cuss and heft

and rattleshatter. What is it
you cannot stand to live with
any longer? Toss it in

and make a wish. Listen—
quarters chime the offertory
platter. Cherries ringing jackpot

from the slots. The dumpster is
an inadvertent music box,
a mausoleum-portalet—

you deposit what you cannot bother
hoping to forget. Roll the stone away
this time next week, the tomb will be

untenanted. Nothing full of possibility
like emptiness. You can start again.
When there is nothing to be salvaged

of the day, bring it here. Heave it
to the asphalt if you have to.
Leave it in the car, and leave the car.

The noise that you are making
is the song I'll wake up wishing
I remembered all the words to.

I am trying to sing it back to you.

Hoverflies

November grins her best impression
of September—warm enough to swim!—
except her light at noon is long
and the water pooled atop the falls
is cold. *So cold,* our son says, almost two,
and imitating you. His shirt and shoes,
his shorts and socks are sunning
on the rocks. Our miniature
skinny-dipper, giddy for the rush
of rosy feet—sting made sugary
by trust of warmth to come.
How can I say I wish this wouldn't end,
when the aching of the moment's leaving
gives the wish its breath?
He slides on algaed slicks.
He scatters tiny fish
and water striders.
Maybe thirty minutes pass
or pool, what minutes do
before slipping from the falls
in mid-November. I scramble down
the shale to gather up his clothes,
stopping when I see—
not yellowjackets—
hoverflies—sentineled above each article,
steady as the minnow
that doesn't know it's watched.
Ringed in black and yellow,

the flies shiver their fly-wings
furiously, silently,
not trying to be anything
but flies. Burning
to be still. Patient
for the absences
we practice, fragrant
with our moisture
and our salt.

"Close Your Eyes" on page 3: The final lines are inspired by the editor's note of Percy A. Morris, *A Field Guide to Shells of the Atlantic and Gulf Coasts and West Indies*, 3rd ed., by Percy A. Morris (Boston: Houghton Mifflin, 1973).

"Dance Lessons" on page 5: References "London Homesick Blues," written by Gary P. Nunn and popularized by Jerry Jeff Walker on his 1973 album *¡Viva Terlingua!*

"Abraham Binds Isaac" on page 13: Owes its form and first line to A. E. Stallings's poem "Olives." "Venison" is the poem's quasi-anagrammatic subject.

"Goliath" on page 19: The subject's persona draws from theologian Howard Thurman's *Jesus and the Disinherited* (Beacon Press, 1996), which examines the degradation of those harmed or killed—not as formidable adversaries, but with "contemptuous disregard for [their] personhood."

"Rodeo" on page 20: Recalls a scene from the Angola Prison Rodeo in 2009. Over five thousand people are incarcerated at Angola State Penitentiary, an eighteen-thousand-acre prison farm located on a former plantation in West Feliciana Parish, Louisiana. The event draws up to ten thousand daily spectators.

"The Orchid and the Wasp" on page 27: Includes an epigraph from "Flowering," the third episode of the BBC miniseries *The Private Life of Plants*, which originally aired January 25, 1995.

"Figure Study" on page 31: Is informed by a profile from the January 1, 1927, issue of the *New Yorker*, in which Janet Flanner writes, "Isadora [Duncan] appeared as a half-clothed Greek. . . . She was the first artist to appear uncinctured, barefooted and free. . . . She came like a figure from the Elgin marbles." Duncan was killed in 1927 when her scarf caught in the rear axle of an Amilcar CGSS convertible. The poem's second line is an interpretation of *The Iliad*, Book 5, line 379, wherein Aphrodite's "immortal robes" are torn by Diomedes. The final lines reference the Winged Victory of Samothrace.

"Infernal Dactyls" on page 32: The first references Virgil's *Georgics*, in which the poet wrote of portentous weather following Caesar's assassination. The second references Acts 1:18.

"*Hippocampus spp.*" on page 34: Refers to the genus of teleost (bony finned) fishes encompassing seahorses. The hippocampus is also a region of the temporal lobe associated with learning and memory, named for its resemblance to a seahorse.

"Found on Google Street View" on page 38: Was written after toggling the "Time Machine" function on the popular web application at the specified intersection.

"Screen" on page 40: The final line echoes William Carlos Williams's "Asphodel, that Greeny Flower."

"Recalling Yeats, Learning of the Mass Shootings in El Paso and Dayton, Rocking Our Son Back to Sleep" on page 41: Specifically recalls the Irish poet's "A Cradle Song." On August 4, 2019, ten people were killed in a mass shooting in Dayton, Ohio. This followed less than a day after twenty-three people were killed in a shooting at a Wal-Mart in El Paso, Texas.

"Squeamish" on page 44: Includes an allusion to "The Hearse Song," a children's rhyme of unknown origin. The poem concludes with a borrowed refrain common in Exodus and Deuteronomy.

"Notes on an Inscription" on page 51: Follows a 2018 visit to the Equal Justice Initiative's National Memorial for Peace and Justice, and time spent at the public archives in Hallettsville, Texas, searching for records surrounding any of the three men identified as lynching victims from Lavaca County. Microfilm of the *Hallettsville Herald* from June 14 and June 21, 1894, identified "Lou" and Will Hall among the youths involved in an altercation that led to the fatal injury of Albert McElroy. The *Herald* makes no indication of arrests, or of Cook's involvement whatsoever. Also on June 14, the *Weekly Chieftan* of Venita, Oklahoma, indicates that Lon Hall and Bascom Cook were arrested and extrajudicially hanged. Excerpts from the *Herald* and *Chieftan* are italicized. On Valentine's Day, 1895, a blizzard hit coastal Texas and the Gulf South. The poem's final stanza references a line from Rilke's "Archaic Torso of Apollo," translated by Stephen Mitchell.

"Casting the Stone" on page 58: Alludes to Charles Lyell, author of *Principles of Geology* (1830–1833), in which he asserts the earth has been shaped by dynamic processes still at work.

"Notes Recovered from a Search for Sanctity" on page 59: Explores a letter documented in *The Abbey of Gethsemani: Place of Peace and Paradox* by Dianne Aprile (Trout Lily Press, 1998). The abbey historian has no other record of the man identified as Able. The poem's first epigraph is taken from Merton's poem in *A Man in the Divided Sea* (1946) and printed in *The Collected Poems of Thomas Merton* (New Directions, New York: 1977) with the accompanying text, "On entering the Monastery of Our Lady of Gethsemani, 1941." The opening lines of the author's poem are taken from Genesis 4:8.

"Beloved Gray Whale Dies after Fifty-Three Days in the Klamath River" on page 47: Takes its title from an August 16, 2011, blog post on *petethomasoutdoors.com*. The whale and her calf were first seen in the river on June 23, 2011. Following efforts to divert the whale back to the ocean, and accompanying national media coverage, the whale died on August 9, 2011.

"When I Miss You in My Sleep" on page 68: References "ivory dreams" as interpreted by Penelope in *The Odyssey* (note that these quotations may vary slightly based on translation): "Two gates there are for our evanescent dreams, one is made of ivory, the other made of horn. Those that pass through the ivory cleanly carved are will-o'-the-wisps, their message bears no fruit" (Book 19, lines 633–636). "A burying of oars" suggests the final prophecy Odysseus receives: "When another traveler falls in with me and calls that weight across my shoulder a fan to winnow grain, then, he told me, I must plant my oar in the earth . . ." (Book 23, lines 313–315). "Strange woman" and "Strange man" are the titles Odysseus and Penelope use for one another following the former's return to Ithaca (Book 23, lines 186 and 193).

"The Dumpster Fillers" on page 70: The final line is inspired by Craig Arnold's poem "Bird-Understander."

Born and raised in Austin, Texas,
Josh Dugat lives with his wife and
children in Tuscaloosa, Alabama.

Kate Light, *Character Shoes: Poems*

April Lindner, *This Bed Our Bodies Shaped: Poems*

David Livewell, *Pass and Stow: Poems*

Susan McLean, *Daylight Losing Time: Poems*

Martin McGovern, *Bad Fame: Poems*

Jeredith Merrin, *Cup: Poems*

Richard Moore, *Selected Poems;*
The Rule That Liberates: An Expanded Edition: Selected Essays

Richard Newman, *All the Wasted Beauty of the World: Poems*

Alfred Nicol, *Animal Psalms: Poems*

Deirdre O'Connor, *The Cupped Field (Able Muse Book Award for Poetry)*

Frank Osen, *Virtue, Big as Sin (Able Muse Book Award for Poetry)*

Alexander Pepple (Editor), *Able Muse Anthology;*
Able Muse: A Review of Poetry, Prose & Art (semiannual, winter 2010 on)

James Pollock, *Sailing to Babylon: Poems*

Aaron Poochigian, *The Cosmic Purr: Poems; Manhattanite (Able Muse Book Award for Poetry)*

Tatiana Forero Puerta, *Cleaning the Ghost Room: Poems*

Jennifer Reeser, *Indigenous: Poems; Strong Feather: Poems*

John Ridland, *Sir Gawain and the Green Knight (Anonymous): Translation;*
Pearl (Anonymous): Translation

Kelly Rowe, *Rise above the River (Able Muse Book Award for Poetry)*

Stephen Scaer, *Pumpkin Chucking: Poems*

Hollis Seamon, *Corporeality: Stories*

Ed Shacklee, *The Blind Loon: A Bestiary*

Carrie Shipers, *Cause for Concern (Able Muse Book Award for Poetry)*

Gabriel Spera, *Twisted Pairs: Poems*

Matthew Buckley Smith, *Dirge for an Imaginary World (Able Muse Book Award for Poetry)*

Susan de Sola, *Frozen Charlotte: Poems*

Barbara Ellen Sorensen, *Compositions of the Dead Playing Flutes: Poems*

Rebecca Starks, *Time Is Always Now: Poems; Fetch, Muse: Poems*

Sally Thomas, *Motherland: Poems*

Paulette Demers Turco (Editor), *The Powow River Poets Anthology II*

Rosemerry Wahtola Trommer, *Naked for Tea: Poems*

Wendy Videlock, *Nevertheless: Poems; The Dark Gnu and Other Poems;*
Slingshots and Love Plums: Poems; Wise to the West: Poems

Richard Wakefield, *A Vertical Mile: Poems; Terminal Park: Poems*

Gail White, *Asperity Street: Poems*

Chelsea Woodard, *Vellum: Poems*

Rob Wright, *Last Wishes: Poems*

www.ablemusepress.com

www.ingramcontent.com/pod-product-compliance
Lightning Source LLC
Chambersburg PA
CBHW021339060726
47591CB00006B/2093